SEAN MATHIAS

INFIDELITIES

AMBER LANE PRESS

For Ian

All rights whatsoever in this play are strictly reserved and application for performance, etc. must be made before rehearsal to:
Margaret Ramsay Ltd.
14a Goodwin's Court
St. Martin's Lane
London WC2N 4LL

No performance may be given unless a licence has been obtained.

First published in 1986 by
Amber Lane Press Ltd.
9 Middle Way
Oxford OX2 7LH

Typeset in Ehrhardt by
Oxford Computer Typesetting

Printed and manufactured in Great Britain by
Cotswold Press Ltd., Oxford

CHARACTERS

JANINE KEAN:	Mid-forties.
JEFFREY (her husband):	A little younger.
MICHAEL:	Late twenties.
MARK:	Mid-twenties.

Infidelities was first presented at the Edinburgh Festival, at the Scottish Centre, on 11th August 1985. It was produced by T. Flynn Productions Ltd. and directed by Richard Olivier, with the following cast:

JANINE: .... Jill Bennett
JEFFREY: .... Peter Kelly
MICHAEL: .... Michael Shaw
MARK: .... Jason Carter

Designed by: Brien Vahey and Marjoke Henrichs
Lighting by: Peter Warde

The production transferred to the Donmar Warehouse, London, on 7th October 1985, as part of the 'Perrier Pick of the Fringe' season.

A new production of *Infidelities* opened at the Boulevard Theatre, London, on 26th June 1986. It was presented by Off the Avenue and directed by Sean Mathias, with the following cast:

JANINE: .... Jill Bennett
JEFFREY: .... John Castle
MICHAEL: .... Michael Shaw
MARK: .... Lucien Taylor

Designed by: Geoff Rose
Lighting by: Rick Fisher

SCENE ONE

A West Hampstead ground-floor flat. A Tuesday afternoon.

The front door opens from outside. Enter JANINE.

JANINE: Come in, won't you? My home.
          [*Enter* MICHAEL.]

MICHAEL: Thank you. Yeah.

JANINE: Of course, it isn't luxurious, but I think tasteful, don't you? A smattering of Habitat makes all the difference, don't you find? Would you care for coffee? Before... these are my African violets. My little darlings, I call them. Aren't you my little darlings? Your feet must be sore. Traipsing about. Remove your shoes. Feel at ease. I'm sorry, was it yes to coffee?

MICHAEL: Yeah. I wouldn't mind a cup.

JANINE: Good. I always feel coffee helps one to relax, don't you? I enjoy West Hampstead. Lived in this flat for many a year. Fixed rent. Are you familiar with it?

MICHAEL: What?

JANINE: West Hampstead.

MICHAEL: No, I'm a South London man. Originated Littlehampton. But I'm a South Londoner now.

JANINE: Really? What were you doing in this part of the world?

MICHAEL: I'd come for an interview.

JANINE: Seeking employment, are you? There's a lot of that going on. I work part-time myself. Dinners at the local primary school. It isn't taxing work. Sit in this chair, won't you? It's a most comfortable one. We recently had it redecorated. A younger woman arrived, with her own machine. She travels in the Central London area. Sit in it, won't you? I'm sorry, what was your name?

MICHAEL: Michael...Michaels. Michael Michaels, yeah.

JANINE: Yes, of course. And I'm Janine. Janine Kean.

MICHAEL: Yeah, I know. I remembered.

JANINE: Yes, you're sharper than me. You have a memory for such things. I'm afraid I ramble rather a lot. I tend to miss certain facts. It's the result of a solitary childhood. My parents, you know, were unable to produce more. We lived in a neighbourhood of elderly people. Old folk. Consequently I was alone with my imagination. I developed a habit of talking to myself. Old habits die hard, wouldn't you say, Mr. Michaels?

MICHAEL: Yeah. I suppose they do. Yeah.

JANINE: You, on the other hand, are obviously the strong silent type. In control of things. I like a man who's balding. I have always been partial to a smooth crown. [*stroking his head*] I should see to the refreshment.

MICHAEL: Oh, that's all right, really, that's quite all right.

JANINE: No, I'll frighten you off. I must exercise more control. I live too much inside my own head. Now then, coffee?

MICHAEL: Yeah. Thank you.

[JANINE *enters the kitchenette part of the living room.*]

JANINE: Don't you find this attractive? It's one of my favourite features. We, of course, installed it. Open plan living, they call it. Just like in the supplements. 'A Room of my Own', 'A Day in the Life of...', 'Relative Values', you know. I find those pages most attractive. Of course, it would be unhealthy to model one's life on magazines, wouldn't it?

MICHAEL: Yeah. Quite wrong, I'd say.

JANINE: I'm particularly fond of my framed posters. Picked that idea up in 'Ideal Home'. Listen to me going on. You must think me an awful hostess. Take your shoes off. Let your pegs breathe.

[MICHAEL *takes his shoes off.*]

That's right. You relax. I'll massage your toes in a sec. Would you care for a biscuit? Breakaway or Garibaldi?

MICHAEL: No thanks, no.

JANINE: Go on. Special offer at Sainsbury's. 3p off the pack. Be tempted.

MICHAEL: No, really. Bit of a gut. Too much bitter.

JANINE: Oh, you boys! You don't have to tell me. But you'll take sugar in your coffee, won't you? Let me guess! Let me guess! You'll take...three.

MICHAEL: That's right!

JANINE: I'm sensitive to these things. Do you take interest in the horoscopes? I'm Pisces. It's a lovely sign. I'm ever so fond of it. I've always been Pisces. But you. Well, I wouldn't mind betting. No, I wouldn't mind betting at all... Capricorn?

MICHAEL: Yeah! That's right!

JANINE: I have a third eye, don't I? I'm funny in that way. Here. Drink this.

[*She brings in coffee for two, then sits on the floor.*]

MICHAEL: Thank you.

JANINE: You have nice feet. I'd reckon size nines.

MICHAEL: Eight and a half, actually.

JANINE: Close though, wasn't I? I like your socks.

[*removing them*] A sort of mustard colour. Attractive. You have personality to wear socks of such a colour. A quiet charisma.

> [*She massages his toes. He almost spills his coffee.*]

MICHAEL: Oh, I'm sorry!

JANINE: No! You're nervy, that's all. We both are. You can tell we're not the promiscuous type. Don't worry! If it had spilt I'd have been cross. That chair's the newly decorated one. I'm fond of that cloth. Sent away to 'Woman's Own'. But there's no harm. You're ticklish, that's all. A shy sort. Capricorn. Mind you, steady as well. Capricorns move slowly in the right direction. Haven't you hairy legs? Most masculine.

MICHAEL: It's only to be expected.

JANINE: Course! I meant no harm. It's just that what with so little hair on your head it came as a surprise, that was all. I bet your chest is of a similar nature. Hirsute is the word, isn't it? Hirsute is what you are. What was the interview?

MICHAEL: Removal Man.

JANINE: Is that your occupation?

MICHAEL: Done it before but I trained as a landscape gardener.

JANINE: How romantic. Oh, I am impressed.

MICHAEL: It's impossible to find such employment. I take any interviews the Job Centre will offer. Yeah.

JANINE: How rotten. How unfair. You have gardeners' hands. Put down your coffee. I'll massage your hands. They're beautiful. Hands which have worked the earth. Hands of experience.

MICHAEL: That's why I was in the park. Strolling.

JANINE: I love that park. It has such pretty gardens. Have you worked them?

MICHAEL: No. This is not my side of the city. I came for the interview.

JANINE: [*remembering*] The removal interview. Go well, did it?

MICHAEL: Promising. Yeah.

JANINE: I'm a silly girl. I don't listen. That's a perfect example of my childhood isolation. You like that park?

MICHAEL: I've been there before, yeah. It's a good park.

JANINE: Secure employment there. You'd be close by. We could meet of a free afternoon. I would massage your extremities.

MICHAEL: You're an attractive woman. Yeah.

JANINE: Thank you. Did you notice me in the park?

MICHAEL: Not immediately.

JANINE: I did. I noticed you immediately. I had gone into the park to break the tedium of the day. I often go in there for that purpose. I should, by rights, be at Sainsbury's now. This is my afternoon for the weekly shop. I noticed you at once. I thought, he's got presence.

MICHAEL: Thank you.

JANINE: You do have presence. I can tell by massaging you.

MICHAEL: Thank you.

JANINE: Were you shocked when I approached?

MICHAEL: I was very pleased. I found you pretty.

JANINE: It isn't often I get told that. Did you enjoy your coffee?

MICHAEL: Oh, yeah. Yeah. Thanks.

JANINE: Care for more?

MICHAEL: Oh, no. No. That was fine.

JANINE: And what did I say?

MICHAEL: When?

JANINE: When I approached. Mind you, I'd seen you winking.

MICHAEL: Yeah. You said, "It's such a pretty day, isn't it? Aren't we lucky in such a big city to have such a pretty green space?" Yeah.

JANINE: That sounds silly.

MICHAEL: No no. It was a pretty thing to say. That's when I thought you were pretty.

JANINE: Still think I am?

MICHAEL: Course. Wouldn't have changed me mind in an hour. You're very pretty.

JANINE: I'm not always doing this, you know. Picking up strangers, you know. In fact, I'm not ever doing it, really.

MICHAEL: I'm not a stranger. Not now.

[He leans forward and kisses her.]

JANINE: You kiss in a Capricorn fashion. A passionate fashion.

MICHAEL: Your tongue is nice. Tastes good. Yeah.

JANINE: Now you're getting excited. You're starting to bulge. You ought to wear more discreet trousers. I noticed that in the park. Your trousers were tight when you was natural. Now that you're starting to bulge they're positively overstated.

MICHAEL: It's not my sex. It's the beer. My clothes are getting tight. Besides, you're an attractive woman.

JANINE: I'm older than you, mind.

MICHAEL: I know. That's why you're attractive. To me. I like the older woman. I think you're lovely. I'm sorry if I've been nervy. I'm not used to this, see. Normally I go out with my mate. Jace. He pulls the birds for me. Does the chatting up. He's got the charm. I like them older. He pulls them, see. Yeah.

[*Pause.*]

Sorry, I didn't mean to ramble.

JANINE: We'd better see to you, hadn't we? Come along, let's go into the bedroom. You most definitely have hands familiar with the earth. You don't want to do Removals. Poking your nose into other folks' homes. Shifting their grubbies.

MICHAEL: It's a skill, mind. A real skill. Here, take this room. Stand on this.

[*He takes a tape measure from his pocket. He places* JANINE *at one end of the room, puts the tape under her foot, and walks with the tape to the other end.*]

Oh, yes. Oh, yes.

[*He does the same across the width of the room.*]

Oh, yes. Oh, yes. Sofa. Table. Chairs. Hi-fi. Telly. Oh, yes. I could shift this flat in two hours. You ever moving on, look me up.

JANINE: Oh, I am impressed. You took on quite a new persona. Very managerial. But you're not the sort to work indoors. Get back to the land. You want to work that park. Visit me on Tuesdays. When I've finished them dinners. These things can be arranged. This way, Michael. I'm looking forward to my experience with you. This way.

[*She opens the bedroom door.*]

This is the bedroom. Go through. And that door next door is the bathroom. You'll be needing that when you've finished your activities. Go through. Don't be shy. I'll just lay out a fresh face flannel, then I'll be through. Don't allow things to subside. Do you like the Beatles? I'll put on a tape. Then we'll get on. You'll have to go before six. I'll put on a tape.

[*She puts on the Beatles.*]

[*The lights fade to black.*]

SCENE TWO

The Beatles fade away. The room is still dark.

JEFFREY: That was wonderful. Quite wonderful. Quite, quite wonderful. You're superb. Sexy. Beautiful. A child's body. That was wonderful.

[JEFFREY *has now entered that same living room from that same bedroom. He switches on the lights.*]

I'll have a fag.

[MARK *enters, half naked.*]

MARK: You just did.

JEFFREY: Funny, too. A sense of humour. An important quality after sex. That was great sex.

[*He kisses* MARK.]

MARK: Thanks.

JEFFREY: No, thank you. You're terrific. Cigarette?

MARK: Thanks. You often go to that toilet?

JEFFREY: Not often. Sometimes the one at Hyde Park Corner. Yes! Of a Tuesday evening. When my wife goes out. Her night out with some friend. Another woman... The cinema. Wine bars. I don't know where. Every Tuesday, she goes out. Leaving me home with the telly. So, sometimes I nip out. Troll down the Finchley Road. That's the word, isn't it? Troll?

MARK: Something like that. How old are you?

JEFFREY: Turned forty. And you?

MARK: Twenty-three.

JEFFREY: God, you're beautiful. Are you bisexual?

MARK: Why, thinking of a threesome with your missus?

JEFFREY: Last thing on my mind. We have no sex play. No intercourse. It's an arid relationship. Arid extra dry.

MARK: Stops you from sweating.

JEFFREY: No danger of sweating with my old lady. Infertile. Let's have some more wine.

> [*He takes a half-drunk bottle of white wine from a side table and pours two glasses. He hands one to* MARK.]

MARK: You wanted children?

JEFFREY: Desperately. That's when I started cottaging. Never slept with a bloke before that. She couldn't produce children. End of relationship.

MARK: And now?

JEFFREY: Now I pick up the occasional lovely boy. None more so than you.

> [*He kisses* MARK.]

MARK: Stop it. Are you a paedophile?

JEFFREY: No, I'm an opportunist.

MARK: What do you do?

JEFFREY: All sorts.

MARK: I mean for a living.

JEFFREY: Well, let's just say I'm a street-walker.

MARK: You mean I gotta pay?

JEFFREY: No! With you, no! Though most have to pay. We all have to pay for our crimes in life, Mark. And what about you?

MARK: What?

JEFFREY: Your living?

MARK: Unemployed.

JEFFREY: I see. It's rife. Hazard of the modern western world. You spend a lot of time in toilets?

MARK: No! Clubs, pubs too. I float around. That room, that where you sleep with your wife?

JEFFREY: It is. The marital bed.

MARK: Will she sleep there tonight?

JEFFREY: Yes.

MARK: How tacky. Won't she smell the sheets? The smell of boys?

JEFFREY: Doubt it. Those sheets come from Habitat. Manufactured from a material that won't allow smells to linger. Besides, she doesn't have those sort of nostrils. She's a woman of untrained temperament.

MARK: Who does she sleep with?

JEFFREY: Me, of course.

MARK: Apart from that.

JEFFREY: I'm sure I don't know. Her best friends' husbands, I would think.

MARK: Don't you ask?

JEFFREY: No, never. The answers would bore me. Her vaginal movement is something which holds no interest for me.

MARK: Sounds gross.

JEFFREY: It is. Believe you me, it is.

MARK: Why didn't you adopt?

JEFFREY: What is this? Mastermind?

MARK: 'scuse.

JEFFREY: No, that's all right. I'm surprised you're interested. She's too neurotic to house another woman's infant.

MARK: Maybe she's a lesbian.

JEFFREY: Doubt it. Her libido would restrict her in that direction.

MARK: Do what?

JEFFREY: Other women are creatures to whom she may moan. Confide in. Drink gin with. See films. Play bingo. The occasional swim. I cannot imagine her developing a taste for the female nipple. That would be far-fetched. Not to mention indecent. I think it would give us grounds for divorce.

MARK: Why not?

JEFFREY: Enough. More wine? Where do you come from?

MARK: Littlehampton.

JEFFREY: Littlehampton? How rural.

MARK: How coastal.

JEFFREY: Yes! I once went there. To Littlehampton.

MARK: What for?

JEFFREY: An outing. Oh, nothing. It was nothing. It was years ago. You'd have been a little boy.

MARK: Well, years ago I would have, yes.

JEFFREY: I'm so glad we met. [*Pause.*] What brought you to London?

MARK: Dunno.

JEFFREY: The big city?

MARK: Suppose.

JEFFREY: In search of fortune? Or maybe love?

MARK: Suppose.

JEFFREY: Did you find either?

MARK: Not so far.

JEFFREY: Don't despair. Twenty-three still qualifies as a young age. Though only just in this era. Get a job. Have you a trade?

MARK: I got two A-levels.

JEFFREY: Excellent. In which subjects?

MARK: English and Art.

JEFFREY: Excellent! You could be a sign-writer. There must be marvellous scope for such learning. You exist on the Welfare State?

MARK: That's about it.

JEFFREY: Find employment. Don't give up. Push on. You must be tough in the city. Visit me. Please. We could frolic on a regular basis. My body isn't bad. I shave daily. I'll give you food and drink under this roof. Help with your tube fares. Will you come again?

MARK: If you like.

JEFFREY: Very much. Very much. I'll put on some music. You'll have to go soon. My wife will return. I'll help with your tube fares. Do you like the Beatles?

[MARK *shrugs and turns up his nose.*]

You should be discovering them. A boy of your age. They're part of our culture. I'll help you toward them.

[*He puts on the Beatles.*]

I'll never forget when 'She Loves You' first come out. You'd have been a toddler. Your Dad would have been about my age. And when it come out I was feeling over the hill. Oh, I was only young, really, but I don't know, I was feeling old for the first time in my life. Then I heard the Beatles. And I felt young again. They made me feel young. Of course, I was too old by rights to be one of their young fans. Like the teenagers. But they made me feel young. I've been listening to them ever since. Nowadays it's not the same. It's all synthesizers. And too many words.

[JEFFREY *is rather startled by his sudden*

honesty. He turns his attention back to
MARK.]
You're a beautiful boy. You'll get on. Another
half-hour then you must go. We can make this
regular. Get to enjoy Tuesdays.
>*[They return to the bedroom.]*
>*[The lights fade to black.]*

SCENE THREE

The music fades and the lights come up.
JANINE *enters through the front door.*

JANINE: Cooee. I'm back. All clear, is it? I've brought
you a Cherry B.
>*[She puts two miniature cherry brandies on*
>*the kitchen counter, takes off her coat, and*
>*hangs it in the closet.]*
This closet could do with a good spring-clean. I
could spend some time in this closet. Go
through it with a fine tooth comb.
>*[She closes the closet door.]*
Fancy a Cherry B?
>*[*JEFFREY *enters in his dressing-gown.]*
JEFFREY: You're back, then.
JANINE: Oh, I say, in your night attire. Feeling snoozy?
JEFFREY: Heavy day. Most satisfactory. Pleasant evening?
You look nice. Rosy cheeks.
JANINE: The walk along the High Street. Most invigor-
ating. Fancy a Cherry B?
JEFFREY: What a treat. My old Mum's favourite. You
used to bring her Cherry B's in Barnes.

JANINE: Sucking up.
[*She laughs. She prepares their drinks.*]
I thought the way to a man's heart is via Mum's tum.

JEFFREY: You were right there. She fell for you hook, line and sinker.
[*They settle to their drinks.*]

JANINE: I was never quite refined enough for her. She was so posh.

JEFFREY: Yes, we was brought up proper.

JANINE: Were, Jeffrey, were. Your grammar's fallen from grace. You used to be so well-spoken. It's your workmates. They encourage lazy speech.

JEFFREY: I was an Eleven-plus star.

JANINE: You were also an only child.

JEFFREY: Correct.

JANINE: So what do you mean, 'we was brought up proper'?

JEFFREY: Figure of speech. You are rosy-cheeked.

JANINE: That'll be the Cherry B.

JEFFREY: Nice evening?

JANINE: Katie. She droned on a bit, you know. Pretty rosy-cheeked yourself. Feeling flush?

JEFFREY: Solitary evening. Me and the telly.

JANINE: Anything good on?

JEFFREY: Just a bit of Wildlife. Katie well?

JANINE: On about her and Keith. How they never do it any more. How their marriage is a shambles.

JEFFREY: I can't think what keeps them together. They've got nothing in common. Not like us.

JANINE: No, not like us. Cheers.

JEFFREY: Cheers. This Cherry B's a real treat. Thank you.
[*He kisses her.*]

JANINE: Oh, I say. Thank you. I love Tuesdays.

JEFFREY: Me too.

JANINE: The break from each other does us the world of good, don't you find?

JEFFREY: Most definitely. Definitely stimulating. Absence makes the heart grow fonder.

JANINE: [*giggling*] Oh, I say. Wish I'd gone in for a few more miniatures, now.

JEFFREY: [*singing*] 'It's the right one. It's the bright one. Cherry Beee...eee!'

[*He gives* JANINE *a cuddle.*]

JANINE: Oh, you're all merry and gay.

JEFFREY: Bit of a cuddle never did anyone any harm. That's what my Mum used to say.

JANINE: God rest her soul. I miss her.

JEFFREY: I miss Barnes. Miss her bubble baths. Why won't you buy me bubble bath? I always have to use Fairy Liquid. I miss her treats.

JANINE: Miss her cash, you mean.

JEFFREY: Now then!

JANINE: How did we ever get through that lot?

JEFFREY: Habitat! Ah, well. Mustn't harp. Fancy a glass of wine before we turn in?

JANINE: Don't mind if I do.

[JEFFREY *prepares some wine.*]

JEFFREY: Fancy listening to a bit of Beatles?

JANINE: Oh, I say, Jeffrey, my favourite.

JEFFREY: Go on, put on a tape.

JANINE: Do you think I ought?

JEFFREY: Go on.

JANINE: How romantic. You've taken on a whole new persona. Very reminiscent.

JEFFREY: Go on, put on the Beatles. Life's full of funny turns.

[JANINE *puts on the Beatles.*]

JANINE: I'll never forget when you first played me 'She Loves You'.

JEFFREY: I'll never forget when it first come out.

JANINE: I'll never forget when we first did the Twist.

[JEFFREY *hands her some wine. He starts to twist.*]

Oh, I say. What a treat. I love treats.

JEFFREY: I love the Twist.

[JANINE *starts to twist.*]

JANINE: Oh! A quick Twist. Then we must turn in.

JEFFREY: Yeah. After all, tomorrow is another day. Yeah. Yeah. Yeah.

[*The lights fade on them both, twisting away.*]

SCENE FOUR

The music fades and morning light comes up on the same room.

JANINE: [*from the bedroom*] See you at six, then. Cheerio.

[*An outside door slams.* JEFFREY *has gone to work.* JANINE *enters.*]

It was chancy meeting that Michael yesterday. He's a most effective young man. I am looking ahead. Almost longingly. I must walk in the park today. Throw stale bread to the ducks. I'm their life-line. They rely on me. Anticipation is written across their faces. Oh! I am looking forward to the week ahead. I can't think how I shall contain myself till next Tuesday. I mean, for once, just for once, I've something to look forward to, don't I?

[*The doorbell rings.*]

Who can that be? Some meter-reader or other, I'll wager.

[*She opens the front door to* MICHAEL.]

Oh, Michael. Good heavens. Come in. What is it? I was just muttering to myself that I was looking forward.

[MICHAEL *enters.*]

MICHAEL: Yeah. I got that job.

JANINE: What job?

MICHAEL: One I went for. Removals.

JANINE: How disappointing.

MICHAEL: No, it isn't. I'm relieved. I need the money.

JANINE: But I shan't be able to see you. To have fun.

MICHAEL: I know. That's why I've come. Yeah.

JANINE: We can't frolic now. I've not the time.

MICHAEL: No. I've come to say I can't meet you next Tuesday.

JANINE: Oh, I am disappointed. Almost enraged. No rendezvous?

MICHAEL: Not Tuesday afternoon. One evening maybe? Yeah.

JANINE: Out of the question. I'm a woman of married status.

MICHAEL: Is your husband in your age group?

JANINE: Roughly. Yes. Why?

MICHAEL: Middling to dark?

JANINE: Yes. Why?

MICHAEL: Enjoys a glass of beer?

JANINE: He likes his food. Why?

MICHAEL: I just seen him.

JANINE: Really? Where?

MICHAEL: Yeah. Leaving this address.

JANINE: That's only natural. He lives here. He exits through that front door each morning.

MICHAEL: I waited for him to leave. Gone to work, has he?

JANINE: Yes.

MICHAEL: For the day?

JANINE: Yes.

MICHAEL: Won't be back till evening?

JANINE: Yes.

MICHAEL: You sure?

JANINE: About what?

MICHAEL: That he won't come back? Gone all day? No reason to come home?

JANINE: Never comes home. Lunches in a caf. Back at six.

MICHAEL: You sure?

JANINE: Certain. Why?

MICHAEL: I'm attracted to you. Let me kiss you.

JANINE: No. It's too early. Besides, you shall make me late. We all have to work. Besides, you should be fulfilling your post at the Removals. You be careful. You have to work hard to hold down a job. You'll be seeing your cards. You need qualities to hold a position. Reliability. Punctuality. Discipline. You seem to show no inclination towards such qualities.

MICHAEL: I'm a reliable man. I was assistant prefect at the orphanage.

JANINE: You a prefect? I'd no idea. You an orphan? I'm amazed.

MICHAEL: I loved it there. Got on well, I did. They was good to me there. Oh, never mind that now. I'm reliable, see. Didn't let you down. I came here this morning to inform you that I shall not be able to make love to you this afternoon.

JANINE: Don't let's discuss such things. Don't mention the four-letter word.

MICHAEL: You mean the word love?

JANINE: Don't mention it. You should go.

MICHAEL: Yeah. But I'd like to see you again. I enjoyed yesterday.

JANINE: Don't talk about it. You must go.

MICHAEL: I could meet you of an evening.

JANINE: I've already said that would be inconvenient. Leave me. Leave me a disappointed woman.

MICHAEL: I'm disappointed too! I'm a disappointed man. I'm fond of you, I am. I'd like to come for tea. Call round of a Sunday. I'd like to meet your husband.

JANINE: You've gone soft in the head, you have. You'd best be going.

MICHAEL: I've grown attached.

JANINE: Soft in the head.

MICHAEL: Mark you, whatever happens later I'm genuinely fond.

JANINE: Bordering on the pathetic.
[*She gently pushes him away.*]

MICHAEL: Yeah. A kiss goodbye? Or I hope farewell.

JANINE: You may kiss me in a modest fashion. Then you must leave.
[*They kiss.*]
I'll show you out.

MICHAEL: I'll pop in again then on my way to the Removals.

JANINE: I shouldn't bother. I'm not at my most in the mornings.
[MICHAEL *leaves and* JANINE *shuts the front door. She continues with her housework before preparing to leave for work.*]

Men! They never change. Unreliable. Most inconsiderate. I knew he'd be no different from the rest. I might have known it. Still, it was nice of him to call and let me know. Not to stand me up without a thought. Poor orphan boy an' all. [*checks her watch*] Oh! Look at the time! This type of activity upsets routine. Throws things asunder. It will soon be impossible not to be late. It's shepherd's pie today. Always makes life difficult. Peas strewn across the dining hall floor. And I must deliver the toaster on the way. To the electricals. A morning without toast is like an evening without sunsets.

> [*The doorbell rings.*]

This is ridiculous. It will be the Jehovah people or some man selling Italian paintings. [*turning off the radio*] I shall entertain neither.

> [*She opens the front door to* MARK.]

MARK: Oh, I'm sorry, I…

JANINE: Religion left this neighbourhood a long while since. And I've neither money nor time for foreign artwork. The occasional framed poster but I stop at that.

MARK: I'm sorry?

JANINE: Stop apologising. You're making me late.

MARK: I'm sorry.

JANINE: There you go. Have you many infuriating habits?

MARK: I'm sorry?

JANINE: I'm on the verge of slamming this door in your face, and I'm not, in general, a violent woman.

MARK: I didn't mean to bother you. I was looking for Jeffrey.

JANINE: My husband.

MARK: Ah…yes.

JANINE: Are you a work colleague?

MARK: Not exactly.

JANINE: If you're a Tuesday evening person, I've no desire to meet you. My husband and I have a proper arrangement. Besides, you're about six days too early.

MARK: No, I'm a friend. A friend of Jeffrey's. Your husband. He's been helping me out.

JANINE: You'd better step in and state your business. Be clear and hurried. I'm aiming to leave.

[MARK *enters.* JANINE *shuts the front door.*]

MARK: I don't think I should hurry. I don't believe any of us should hurry. That's what's wrong with the world, innit? Everyone in a tear. Gadding about. You relax.

JANINE: Gadding about! I'm off to work. Are you a warden?

MARK: No. No. I'm an intimate. An intimate of your hubby's.

JANINE: I've no desire for such discussion. I can copy a message and leave it for Jeffrey. Would that suit? What should the message read?

MARK: No. No. You relax. Don't want to go leaving messages about the place. Let's just us have a nice leisurely day.

JANINE: Leisurely, ha! What on earth do you mean? Leisurely. What can you be considering? I'm a dinner lady. I've dinners to oversee. [*laughs*] You're a one!

MARK: He's a nice man, your husband. Fond of him are you? [*Pause.*] I am. [*Pause.*] Aren't you going to offer me a cuppa?

JANINE: You're delaying me. I'm falling behind. If you'll excuse me.

[*She turns to go the bedroom.* MARK *puts the*

chain on the front door. JANINE *turns around.*]

What are you doing?

MARK: I'm spending this evening with your husband. I'm spending the day with you.

JANINE: No! That isn't how it works. We never overlap. Jeffrey's Tuesday evenings are his affair. I have my Tuesday afternoons. We never share rendezvouses. It wouldn't be proper. Permissive sort of behaviour. Besides, today is Wednesday.

MARK: Who mentioned permissive? I simply thought I'd get to know you a little.

JANINE: You trying to usurp me? Pursuing grounds for divorce? [*laughs*] Is that what he told you? [*laughs*] You've been misled. There's to be no divorce in this household. We underwent a Roman Catholic wedding. A thorough process. We stick to our original contract. God may have abandoned us now, but He and His rules exist in our past.

MARK: Haven't you peculiar phrasing? It's almost sweet.

JANINE: I should prefer it if we didn't take this conversation onto a personal plateau. I must ask you to leave. Your business with my husband may be taken up with him directly he returns from his work. Call again then.

MARK: Oh no! It isn't that easy. It's you I want to get to know.

JANINE: I've already informed you, there's no room for divorce here. We're very happy. We each pursue our individual indiscretions. Of a Tuesday. I in the afternoon. He the evening. When I go out. With another female. Why am I telling you all this?

MARK: You need a friend. Someone to confide in. You've found me.

JANINE: I must go. I'll be terribly late. Now where's that toaster?

MARK: Not so fast.

> [*He goes to* JANINE *and grips her by both arms.*]

Now Janine, just you telephone the school and complain of a jibby tummy. A dinner lady with the shits is no good to three hundred starving children.

JANINE: You seem equipped with facts. Quite a range. From my Christian name to the number of pupils at St. David's.

MARK: Don't get smart. Just get on the phone.

JANINE: I don't lie on principle.

MARK: Let's bend your principles a little, then, shall we?

> [*He twists one arm behind* JANINE'*s back. She screams.*]

JANINE: Ow! You're hurting me. That hurts.

MARK: Pick up the receiver and the pain will ease.

JANINE: No. I must go to work. It was lovely meeting you.

> [MARK *forces her arm higher. She screams louder.*]

Ow! All right. All right. Please stop hurting me.

> [*Holding* JANINE *tightly by the wrist* MARK *guides her to the telephone. He releases his grip so that she may dial. He stands close to her and listens in to the earpiece to check the conversation's authenticity.*]

Hello, St. David's? ... Oh, hello, is that Miss Jenkins? ... Hello, Miss Jenkins, Janine Kean here. How are you? ... Janine Kean, Miss

Jenkins. From dinners. Meal supervision divi-
sion. Often bending down of an afternoon to
gather up peas... That's right, Miss Jenkins.
Well, not this afternoon, I'm afraid. No pea
collection for me today... Oh, I've been up half
the night. Poor Jeffrey. He can't have slept a
wink with me. I was that disturbed. Substance
left my every pore. It was awful, Miss Jenkins. I
don't believe I can describe how awful... What?
...No, of course. Thank you, Miss Jenkins, I
shall see you tomorrow. I hope... Goodbye.
          [*She replaces the receiver.*]

MARK: For someone who don't lie, you did OK.

JANINE: It's my imagination. It's boundless. When
encouraged to use it, there seems to be no
stopping me.

MARK: And what does your imagination make of me?

JANINE: I can't think what to make of you. I must say,
your behaviour is queer. And I feel it's rather
rude of you to hold me here against my better
judgement.

MARK: Exciting, too, eh? Could be turned to your
advantage.

JANINE: What could?

MARK: This situation.

JANINE: I fail to see how. Everything seems to conspire
to my disadvantage. I've missed a day from
school. I shan't be able to shop. And I shan't get
into that park. What is it you want here?

MARK: Why is the park so important?

JANINE: I love its space, its greenery, its nature. I find
release there.

MARK: You hope.

JANINE: I'm sorry?

MARK: You hope to find your satisfaction in that park.

JANINE: I'm sorry?

MARK: Stop apologising.

JANINE: I don't know that I fully grasp your meaning.

MARK: Do you think that you could fully grasp me?

JANINE: How impertinent! You're not my idea of a rendezvous.

MARK: Stretch your imagination. Allow your knicker elastic to ride a little.

JANINE: Why is it men always desire dirty talk? Besides, knickers are not part of my present apparel.

MARK: A statement like that is designed to excite.

JANINE: By no means. Those are the bare facts.

MARK: I could provide you with a penetration that you have previously only dreamt of.

JANINE: Please! We ought not to discuss such things. It's still ante-meridian.

MARK: [*slowly and provocatively*] Sex in the mornings is the most welcome sex of all. A slight crusting around the eyelashes. A staleness still on the breath. Beads of perspiration under the pits. A vague emission onto the sheets. Cold feet. These are the morning's associations.

[*He kisses* JANINE *on the neck.*]

JANINE: I must say your dirty talk is quite refined.

MARK: I've had a lifetime's training. I was a poor orphan, you see.

JANINE: How upsetting.

MARK: Let's not go into that now. Let's go into your bedroom. In between your sheets, let's plunge into your mattress.

[*Standing behind* JANINE *he slowly pushes his hand right up her skirt.*]

Let's coil up each spring of your mattress to the

smallest metal band and then release them until they expand further than ever before and your mattress reaches high up towards the ceiling. So high you'll hardly credit it.

> [*At this moment* JANINE *looks close to orgasm.* MARK *abruptly pulls his hand from under her skirt.*]

JANINE: Oh, you're an imaginative boy. You have charisma. It's my favourite quality.

MARK: You like the Beatles?

JANINE: My favourite group.

MARK: Put on a tape. It'll be nice background.

> [JANINE *puts on a Beatles' tape.*]

Follow me. This way. This is the bedroom. This is going to be the most exciting day you ever spent.

> [JANINE *follows him towards the bedroom.*]

JANINE: This is ridiculous. I'm of an age to be your mother.

MARK: Maturity is the better bedfellow.

> [*The bedroom door closes behind them.*]
>
> [*The lights fade to black.*]

SCENE FIVE

The music fades and the lights come up.

JANINE *enters the bedroom. She is wearing a pink quilted housecoat.* MARK *follows.*

JANINE: I've never been through an experience like that. Rather like having a baby.

MARK: Is it?

JANINE: I should imagine. I'm a childless woman.

MARK: No longer, Now you've got me. I could satisfy you constantly.

JANINE: Don't be silly. I'm a woman of married status.

MARK: I could satisfy your old man as well.

JANINE: A menage. How filthy.

MARK: I could be your permanent houseboy. Poor orphan that I am. I'd be like a son to you both.

JANINE: Shut up! That's silly talk. I'm sorry. I didn't mean to shout. I'm overwhelmed by my experience with you. It's made me over-sensitive. The truth is, I couldn't share you.

MARK: And why should you? After all, this flat is small. You'd be unable to escape the sounds of sex occurring between me and hubby. And one can't listen to the Beatles eight days a week!

JANINE: Don't let's talk about my husband. I want to sleep with you again.

MARK: You're direct.

JANINE: I've never said anything like that before. You've changed me. I want that mattress to coil again.

MARK: Let us not hurry. The future of the universe spreads ahead.

JANINE: I want to spread ahead of you. Oh! Now I'm being dirty. I'll put the kettle on. Cup of tea?

MARK: I like this flat. You got nice furniture.

JANINE: All hand-chosen. Fills me with pride.

MARK: I could be very happy here. Pity there's no spare room.

JANINE: Don't be silly. You couldn't stop here. It's a home for a couple. We've only ever lived as a couple.

MARK: No children?

JANINE: That's a raw subject.

MARK: Why?

JANINE: I would have loved a child. Someone to cater for. Jeffrey doesn't care for them. He's a selfish man. He had the op. Sterilised. Without my knowledge or consent. That's the definition of selfish.

MARK: That's not what he said.

JANINE: Well, he's a liar. You don't want to go listening to him.

MARK: Keep your hair on. I was only saying…

JANINE: He's no right to talk to strangers about children.

MARK: I'm sorry. I didn't realise it was taboo. But I wasn't a stranger. We'd just fucked.

JANINE: You're a queer boy.

MARK: He said you was infertile.

JANINE: He's a liar. I'd have longed for children. I'd have considered adoption. It was all a mistake.

MARK: What was?

JANINE: It was all a mess. I'm confused. Please let's go back to bed.

MARK: Not now. If you played your cards right you could have me as a permanent fixture.

JANINE: How?

MARK: Leave him.

JANINE: What?

MARK: Leave your husband.

JANINE: I thought you liked him.

MARK: I prefer women. That's where my inclination really lies. The sample you have tasted could be yours all the time, night and day. Leave him and come with me.

JANINE: Where?

MARK: To bed. Permanently. I'll change your life.

JANINE: I'll bet.

MARK: Go and pack.

JANINE: What?

MARK: Go and pack your things.

JANINE: Now?

MARK: Of course. Life's an adventure. I'll change the course of your destiny. Do you have separate wardrobes? Separate drawers?

JANINE: Completely.

MARK: Good. So he won't notice your things are missing. Leave him a note. Say you've gone out for the evening.

JANINE: What about his tea?

MARK: He'll survive. We all do. Come with me. I'll show you paradise. Life's an adventure. You'll exist in continuous orgasm.

JANINE: Continual.

MARK: That too. Go and pack. Pack it all. Be drastic.

JANINE: I could not pretend it was a happy marriage. I could not feign that pretence. We were always sexually incompatible. Different needs. I've known little sex. I've lived my life with naivety. But this. It's so sudden. I feel suddenly foolish. I should come to my senses.

[*By using his sexuality* MARK *reassures her.*]

MARK: Collect your belongings from the bathroom. Every last hairpin. Get the Kleenex, the cotton buds, your face flannel. All your knickers and tights. Bring your warm things. Some nice towels. Your face creams. Go and pack. You won't regret it.

JANINE: I'm going. I'm going.

MARK: Good.

JANINE: I shall go mad. I don't know what's come over me.

MARK: Only me. Have you some body lotion? I'd like to cream my skin. It's good when it's smooth.

You'd like your baby to stay smooth?
            [MARK *drops his gown.*]
I'll show you paradise.
JANINE: I'll go and pack.
            [*She goes into the bedroom.*]
            [*The lights fade to black.*]

SCENE SIX

The music fades and the lights come up.

MARK *is sitting on the sofa in his jeans, creaming his arms and chest. Quite casually he puts away the lotion and starts to dress.*

JANINE: [*off*] I say. Feels more like I'm moving house than running off for a few days.

  MARK: A few days? Once you're inside my bed you'll need more than a few days.

JANINE: [*off*] I doubt it not. I'm so thrilled chance brought us together.

  MARK: That wasn't chance, darlin'. These things don't happen by chance.

JANINE: [*off*] But it was chance that you met Jeffrey, no?

  MARK: By design. I've been following you both for quite some time now. You to the school. To your dinners. To the shops. The weekly at Sainsbury's. To the newsagent's. Popping in on a Monday to beg the leftover colour supplements from the Sunday papers…

            [MARK *is now dressed.* JANINE *enters from the bedroom. She also is dressed.*]
…Going to the park. Regular visits. Walking round and round them ducks. Them quacking

bills. Pressing your stomach against the wire
netting. Chucking in your stale Mother's Pride.
'Cos your Mother's Pride was always a little bit
stale, wasn't it, darlin'? Getting involved with
the wildlife while always searching for a pick-
up. Searching desperately. You never had
much luck, though you don't half chat to
strangers. That what you mean by naivety? Got
a bloke yesterday, did'n'cha? Saw you bringing
that bloke back here. Fun, was it? Every
Tuesday evening out with a friend, leaving
hubby alone, eh? Pubs. Pictures. Always home
by eleven-twenty. Pictures at the weekend with
hubby. Wandering around Swiss Cottage.
Mingling with the emigrés. A little light local
shopping on a Saturday morn. Once a fortnight
you and hubby splash out and trip off to the
wine bar in the High Street. Paté and French
bread your favourite, isn't it, Janine? Hubby
likes a glass of Chablis. You've taught him
about wines. You read about them in the
magazines. Study the wine club offers. Your
voice don't half carry in public, darlin'. Then, if
you're feeling really exotic, an Indian of a
Saturday night. Bhindi bhaji and a chunk of
nan. Wouldn't throw that to the ducks, wouldja,
gel?
     [Pause.]
JANINE: I don't get it.
  MARK: Missing the point, are we?
JANINE: You've been following me.
  MARK: Dawning, is it? Suddenly brightening?
JANINE: No. Why? What d'you want?
  MARK: Plenty.

[*He puts his hand over her crotch.*]
Plenty, but it don't include that.
[*He spits at her crotch.*]
Vile messy thing. You poor old tart. You'll see.

JANINE: Stop it! Stop this at once!

MARK: There's nothing you can do. You're helpless. Powerless. You'll see.

JANINE: I'm calling the Police. I don't understand. I thought we were going away. What you on about?

MARK: I've been following you for months. For nine whole months. Time it takes a woman to have a baby. That's how long I've been after you.
[*He twists* JANINE's *arms behind her back. She screams. He takes some rope from his back pocket and ties her hands severely behind her.*]

JANINE: Please!

MARK: Now let's shut you up, shall we?
[*He gags her.*]
Well, it's gone five. Hubby'll be home soon. Mustn't let him see you like this, must we? We'll have to hide you away. We'll have to be ashamed of you, won't we? Hide you in the closet. Naughty girl.
[*He slaps her arse.*]
Who's a naughty girl? And when naughty Janine's in the closet, we'll have to rope her legs up, won't we?
[*He slaps her arse again.*]
And now her baby's cross.
[*He slaps her arse again. By now she is frightened and crying.* MARK *leads her to the closet where* JEFFREY's *uniform hung.*]
Into the closet.

[*He forces her into the closet. He ties her legs.*]

Now, Janine, just to show you what a nice sort of boy I am, how decent I am, I'm going to leave this door open so that you can get some air, that is until hubby comes home. All right? Will that be all right for you, Janine? But when hubby comes home, I'm going to have to close this door. I'm sorry, but I'm going to have to. Now, if you bang about and cause a rumpus, which I'll be prepared for, I'll make things very sticky for you. Understand? If you're a good girl, and I know you can be, I feel certain of that, then you won't be in there for long. Not long at all. Understand?

[JANINE *nods.*]

Good. Packed all your stuff?

[JANINE *nods.*]

Good. I'm going to hide your cases under the bed. All right?

[JANINE *nods.* MARK *goes to the bedroom.* JANINE *attempts an escape from the closet. She gets to the front door, then trips and falls.* MARK *enters.*]

What the fuck are you doing? Don't like it in there, do we?

[*He helps her to her feet.*]

I know the feeling. They used to do it at the home. The orphanage. Where I grew up. Lock boys in the closet. Happened to me once. Well, to be honest, more than once. It was filthy. Naturally, I'm discussing the full intellectual experience. Disturbed me ever since. Marked me for life. They left me there for three hours. Fucking bullies. Three hours of solid panic. It was so dark. I was convinced I was choking. Couldn't get no air. There was no room, you see. No room to move about. Just me, my body, and four walls. Three and one door, that is. Locked door. I wasn't tied. I could move my limbs. There was just no room. It was smaller than your closet. I think that's what hell must be like. Something smaller than your closet. And for three hours I never stopped panicking. If I could've got a hard on, could've had a wank. My cock would've touched the door. But I was scared the whole time. I couldn't think about sex. Not ordinary things. I sometimes wake up in the night now, sweating, scared. I hated that place. Ever visited an orphanage? You said you considered adoption. You were better off out of it. Then I got fostered. Down Cardiff. Fourteen, I was. They were called Joany and Bob. They were cunts. Much worse than that orphanage. Ran away. Been running ever since. Now I'm here. You wouldn't want to adopt me, would you, Janine? Listen to me rambling on. It's this bloody cupboard.

[*He guides* JANINE *back to the closet.*]

Brings things back. So, you see, I'm quite sympathetic to your plight. Been through it meself. You with no kids. Me no parents. We've a lot in common. I don't mean to endanger you.

[*There is the sound of a key in the door.*]

Ooops, sorry, darlin'. Must be hubby. Be a good girl and it'll all be over soon.

[*He shuts the closet door.* JEFFREY *enters through the front door.*]

My, you cut a sexy figure in that uniform.

JEFFREY: What the hell are you doing here? Where's my missus?

MARK: She went out.

JEFFREY: Did she let you in? What did you tell her?

MARK: Nothing. Don't panic. I said I worked with you. We'd arranged to meet this evening. For a drink. I'd come round early because I live the other side of London. No time to go home first.

JEFFREY: And she swallowed that?

MARK: She swallowed it all right. She swallowed it.

JEFFREY: So now you know how I earn a living.

MARK: I already knew. Your missus let it out. The traffic warden bit. Asked me how I felt about being a traffic warden. I replied the sadist in me loved it. Your secret's safe with me. Besides, I like a man in uniform.

JEFFREY: Where's she gone? I don't understand.

[MARK *goes to* JEFFREY *and kisses him.*]

MARK: It's all right. She's gone. For the evening. A friend of hers wasn't well. She went to do some shopping for her.

JEFFREY: That'll be Katie.

MARK: She went to keep her company. She trusted me. She was right to.

JEFFREY: No room for alarm. You're a lovely boy.

MARK: Thank you.

JEFFREY: I don't like you seeing me in my uniform.

MARK: It's sexy.

JEFFREY: If only it were a little higher ranking. A bit more class. Are you ashamed of me? We live beyond our means. That's her. She's affected. She has too much imagination. Glass of wine?

MARK: Allow me. In the fridge? You sit down. Relax. You've had a hard day. On the beat.

[*He goes to the kitchen and takes a bottle of screw-top wine from the fridge. He gets two glasses.*]

JEFFREY: Glasses are third on the left. I'm tired. Tired of all this. I should like a change of existence. I'm a disappointed man.

[MARK *opens the wine, pours two glasses and hands one to* JEFFREY.]

MARK: Stick with me. You'll be all right.

JEFFREY: You've blossomed since yesterday. Less shy. You're a nice kid. You sure it was all right with her?

MARK: Positive.

JEFFREY: We lead an odd life. Peculiar habits. She's peculiar all round. She had a nervous breakdown. Years back. Nasty business. We don't mention it.

MARK: She said she wanted to adopt a child.

JEFFREY: That what she told you? She's mad. Stark raving. She hates children.

MARK: Then why does she work at a school?

JEFFREY: Tell you that, did she? Had quite a little chat? She's a right chatterbox. I could use a change.

MARK: Let's go to bed.

JEFFREY: Haven't had a bath.

MARK: Even better. The full taste of your body, fresh off the beat. What could be better?

JEFFREY: You're giving me a hard.

MARK: Good. What could be better? Put on a tape.

JEFFREY: You mean the Beatles?

MARK: Yes.

JEFFREY: You been listening to them?

MARK: Constantly.

JEFFREY: You've positively blossomed. It's as if you've come home. I love the Beatles.

[*He puts on the Beatles.*]
Two nights in a row. That's a real treat. We got
longer tonight on account of your being early.
You've brightened my life.

MARK: Good. I'd like to change things for you.
[*They go into the bedroom.*]
[*The lights fade to black.*]

SCENE SEVEN

The music fades and the lights come up.
MARK *enters, dressing.*

JEFFREY: [*off*] I don't have many things.

MARK: Well, do it. Bung them in a suitcase and we'll
go.
[JEFFREY *appears from the bedroom in a
bold Hawaiian shirt.*]

JEFFREY: It's mad. But I want to. I want to live in bed with
you.

MARK: There's justification in that. I've got appeal.

JEFFREY: Plenty. I'll pack. You've won me over.
[*He disappears into the bedroom.*]

MARK: Good. You won't regret this. Bring everything.
Bung it in cases.

JEFFREY: [*off*] We don't seem to have many cases. I don't
know where she keeps them. Some closet, I
suppose. Still, I've not got much. I was never a
tidy packer.

MARK: Bung it in. Who gives a sod? It'll all come out
the other end. When you've packed, I'm going
to spoil you. We're going to play a little game.
It'll really turn you on. Blow your mind, as they
say.

JEFFREY: [*off*] No drugs. I don't want any involvement.
[*He re-appears.*]
Are you a consumer?

MARK: Of what?

JEFFREY: Drugs.

MARK: Course not. I'm a clean-living boy. That's me. I live by the book.
[JEFFREY *returns to his packing.*]

JEFFREY: Good. You're a good boy. We got to have rules. Rules to abide by.

MARK: Abide by me and I'll see you through.

JEFFREY: [*off*] I've just thought. Where we going to live?

MARK: My place. It's big. Comfortable. I come from a very large family. There's money.

JEFFREY: [*off*] You don't seem like a boy who comes from money.

MARK: Don't restrict your imagination. You don't have to act all public school to come from money. Don't worry. Trust me. Relax. I handled your missus, didn't I?
[JEFFREY *enters with suitcases.*]

JEFFREY: You certainly did. And you certainly seem to be handling me. I'm enjoying it. Makes a nice change.

MARK: Good. Ever been in for S and M?

JEFFREY: What are you on about?

MARK: Bit of bondage.

JEFFREY: You're a one! You're full of bright ideas!

MARK: I'm serious. You watch. I'll tie your hands behind your back and you see how big your old fella goes.

JEFFREY: Sounds daft.

MARK: Harder than ever.

JEFFREY: I'll give it a try.

MARK: Here.

[*He ties* JEFFREY's *hands behind him quite severely.*]

JEFFREY: That's a real boy scout's knot, that is.

MARK: Learnt it at the orphanage.

JEFFREY: You an orphan? You never said. I thought you come from a big family.

MARK: None bigger than the orphanage.

JEFFREY: Well, I'm sorry. You never said.

MARK: You never asked.

JEFFREY: This don't seem to be doing anything for my cock.

MARK: It will. You'll see. There's a surprise for you.

JEFFREY: What? I love treats.

MARK: Go and open that closet door. You'll see.

JEFFREY: Be a bit difficult like this.

MARK: Part of the fun. You'll have to use your elbow.

JEFFREY: You've some imagination. I like that.

[*He opens the closet door, using his tied elbow. He turns to face the closet. There stands* JANINE.]

What the hell?...

[MARK *quickly ropes* JEFFREY's *legs together while he is in a state of shock.*]

What? What the hell?... What are you doing? What's going on here?

[MARK *unties the terrified* JANINE's *gag.*]

JANINE: It's Baby Jason! Jason! Baby Jason!

MARK: Oooh! She's a sharp one, your missus. She doesn't miss much, does she, Dad?

JANINE: Oh Jesus!

JEFFREY: What are you two on about? What's the game here?

JANINE: Oh Jesus! It's him! It's the baby! The baby! It's bloody Jason!

JEFFREY: You! Stop swearing. Now, what is this? Mark,

untie us. What is this, Mark?

MARK: You're not as fast as the old lady, are you, Pop?

JEFFREY: What are you saying?

JANINE: Jesus, it's Jason! Ah! Ah! Ah! I slept with him. He raped me. He forced me. Honest. Ah! Ah! Ah! I let me own son fuck me.

JEFFREY: Shut up, you stupid bitch. You'll have the whole town in here. Now, Mark, what is this? Who are you, son? I mean, who are you?

MARK: We mustn't all panic. Trust me. Things'll turn out for the best.

JEFFREY: Untie us. Untie us, you little bastard!

MARK: No. I shan't. And I'm nobody's bastard.

JANINE: He ain't. He ain't. Oh, fuck.

JEFFREY: Will you keep your stupid female mouth shut? You're going and putting ideas into the boy's head.

[JANINE *attempts to get to the sofa.*]

MARK: Where you going, Ma?

JANINE: Don't! Don't you dare call me that!

MARK: Well, where do you think you're going?

JANINE: I got to sit down. I'm going to drop. I'm on the verge of fainting. I truly am verging.

[*She sits down.*]

JEFFREY: What do you want from us?

[*Pause.*]

MARK: Not much.

JEFFREY: Who are you?

MARK: Your son. The one you give away. Birth Certificate.

[*He produces a birth certificate.* JEFFREY *scrutinises it.*]

JEFFREY: This doesn't mean a thing. You could've stolen it. It could be forged.

[MARK *shakes his head.*]

MARK: St. Theresa's, Littlehampton mean anything?

JEFFREY: Littlehampton, yes. You said before. You mentioned it last week. I never thought. I been there, yes. I blocked it out. But that don't mean...

MARK: That don't mean shit. That don't mean shit. That what you were going to say?

JANINE: It's him, you cretin. Can't you see it's him? It's our boy. I never wanted to give you away, darling. It was him. He was jealous. I was ill. Had a breakdown. Couldn't look after you, see. It was him.

JEFFREY: Stop lying! She used to batter you. She's never known how to handle human beings.

JANINE: That isn't true.

MARK: Shut up! Shut up both of you! I didn't come for that. I don't need your meagre explanations.

JEFFREY: If you're really our boy, we could...we could...

MARK: Oh yeah? [*Pause.*] You could nothing. You're a pair of pond people. Snivelling little pervs. [*Pause.*] I've a knife. Nice little flick-knife. Don't be frightened. I don't intend to harm you. I'm going to untie you. You'll be free. You must do as I say. It'll all be over soon. Now, no trouble. No noise. No attempts at nothing. Or I'll use this. See?

[*He unties* JANINE.]

You shopped me once before. You're going to have to think twice before you shop me once again. I want you to go into the kitchen and pack everything away from them cupboards.

JANINE: Those cupboards were a special offer from MFI. It took me an age to decide between the teak and the white. I think I chose well, don't you?

[*There is a ring at the door.*]
Thank God. Relief.
[MARK *points the knife at* JANINE.]

MARK: Right! You! Open that door! And no funny business. Or he...gets it.
[MARK *points the knife towards* JEFFREY. JANINE *opens the door to* MICHAEL.]

JANINE: Oh, Michael, thank God. [*screaming*] Help!

MARK: Get her in.
[MICHAEL *steps in.*]

MICHAEL: Hello, Janine, all right?

MARK: Shut that bleeding door.

MICHAEL: Hold on, mate, got to get these crates in. Good packing crates these are, mind.
[*He puts down his packing crate.*]
This your husband? How do?
[JEFFREY *ignores him.*]

JANINE: Oh! You're a team! I might have known. I knew you was unreliable.

MICHAEL: No. No. I'm a reliable bloke. I'm his mate. He's always been good to me.

MARK: Leave it, Michael. Untie him.

MICHAEL: Yeah. Course.

JEFFREY: Sweet Jesus! Who is this?

JANINE: It's yesterday's gent.

JEFFREY: What the hell's he doing here?

JANINE: Search me.

JEFFREY: Well, ask him, you silly cow.

JANINE: Excuse me, Michael, my husband wants to know...

MARK: What is this? A double act? I don't consider you two are in much of a position to be demanding answers.

JANINE: Jason, be careful with that knife, darling. Could

be sharp. Could cut yourself.

JEFFREY: How do you know he's Jason?

JANINE: Don't talk daft. He's got your hands. And he's got my smile. Lovely smile.

JEFFREY: Jesus, this is no time to get sentimental.

JANINE: I wish you'd stop blaspheming.

MARK: I wish you'd both shut up. You're getting me down.

MICHAEL: Yeah. They're a right pair of comedians. She likes a good yenter. Mind you, you're a lovely lay.

JANINE: That's vile. In front of our Jace. Literally vile. Be discreet.

JEFFREY: You're nothing but a pair of yobs.

MARK: Shut up! Michael, keep your mouth shut, son. Get started. You two into the kitchen. It's time we started packing.

> [JANINE *and* JEFFREY *go into the kitchen.* MICHAEL *leaves the house with the television.*]

JANINE: Here! What's he doing? Bring that back, you little punk!

MARK: Shut your mouth, Ma. [*pointing the knife*] Or you'll get this right up your clitoris. You attract attention and I'll make trouble. Anyway, what you going to do? Tell the Old Bill? I'm your son. Baby Jason. Whatever happened to Baby Jason? You and hubby just fucked the tits off him, that's what. Go tell that to the Pigs. Now get packing.

> [*They start to pack everything into packing crates.*]

JANINE: Seems such a pity. Some of my best china here. [*holding up a teacup*] This one come from

Habitat. I love Habitat. Such beautiful pieces.
Only thing is, I could never afford complete
sets.

JEFFREY: What are we meant to be doing?

MARK: Packing. Packing.

JEFFREY: Going on a trip, are we?

MARK: Further than you'll ever know, Dad.

> [MICHAEL *enters with two more packing
> crates. He removes an armchair.*]

Tell you what. I'll put on the Beatles. Make a
nice farewell to your stereo.

JEFFREY: This is madness. I'm going to the Police
Station.

JANINE: Be careful. He'll use that knife. Jason was
always a ruthless baby. [*holding up a plate*] I love
this one. Always my favourite plate.

MARK: Go on you, Dad. What you going to tell them?
Go on you. [*holding up the birth certificate*] Start
an inquiry. You're going to lose in the end.

JANINE: Leave it, love. He's right. It's our Jace. We owe
him this much. Mind you, I'll miss this china.

> [JEFFREY *looks resigned.* JANINE *packs away
> their kitchen.* MICHAEL *removes more furn-
> iture.* MARK *puts on the Beatles.*]

> [*The lights fade to black.*]

SCENE EIGHT

The music fades and the lights come up.

*The living room is now bare except for the framed
posters, the stereo, the sofa and the carpet.* JEFFREY
is collapsed on the sofa. JANINE *is taking the posters
off the walls. The kitchen has its cupboard doors*

open, revealing bare shelves. MICHAEL *is removing the last packing crate packed with kitchenware.*

JEFFREY: You'll never get away with this, son.

JANINE: It's a sad job, removals. Having to pack everything away. Moving on. These posters are leaving a nasty stain.

MARK: Leaving their calling card.

JANINE: I don't believe this is happening. You boys taking all our belongings. All.

JEFFREY: They got a van out there.

MARK: A big 'un.

JEFFREY: Stolen, no doubt.

JANINE: Are you really our boy?

MARK: Work it out.

JEFFREY: Don't listen to him. He told me he had two A-levels. His life's full of hoax. He's just a typical orphan boy. The type that invites trouble. He's typical of the type that was brought up without parents.

JANINE: Well, that was our Jason. Our Jason was brought up in that fashion. Without parents.

JEFFREY: If you're our Jason, why are you called Mark?

MARK: Whoever heard of anyone called Jason? "Where's the Argonauts, Jace?" I got a lot of that shit when I wasn't in the cupboard.

JANINE: He is our boy. Look at them eyes.

[MICHAEL *enters, sweating and dirty.*]

MICHAEL: Here, darlin', you've got a lovely arse. How about a little 'ow's your father? Yeah.

JANINE: Get on, I'm due for a rest! I've had to get these things packed up for Jason.

MICHAEL: Well, we had a date. Be nice for us both. Enjoy ourselves.

JANINE: You've a point there.

MICHAEL: I've a point here and all, darlin'.

            [*He puts* JANINE*'s hand on his crotch.*]

JANINE: I say. So you do. Well, if Jason don't mind. You
            don't mind me having a bit of fun for a few
            minutes, do you, Jace? It upset me in that
            cupboard. I'd be happy to wash away the
            memory. And I've earned a break.

MICHAEL: What about your old man?

JANINE: He can't come!

MICHAEL: Does he mind? Yeah.

JANINE: No! He'll be glad to pass some time with Jason.
            Have a paternal chat. Come on.

MICHAEL: I don't want to upset him. You've been good to
            me. I've grown attached. He'll come round to
            me in the end. I'll win him round. I've a way
            with folks. Folks like me. I'd like you to like me.
            The two of you. I'll come round for Sunday tea.

MARK: Stop talking, Michael. On with the task in
            hand.

MICHAEL: Yeah. Good job we saved that bed till last.

            [MICHAEL *and* JANINE *disappear into the
            bedroom.*]

JEFFREY: [*shouting*] She's a slut, that woman! Absolute
            whore! And what you mixing with him for?
            Complete bloody simpleton! You want to get
            yourself some decent mates.

MARK: Let's us have a break, eh? Glass of wine?

            [*He pours two glasses of wine and hands one
            to* JEFFREY.]

JEFFREY: I can tell you something: if, and I stress the
            word if, you are Baby Jason, then I'm not your
            father anyway. I never slept with her. Not ever.
            She's older than me, mind. She's the older
            woman. We were at the same school, but she

was on the shelf. She's older, you see. We never did much sleeping. When we were newly married she wouldn't do it. Said she was shy. Give her time. We messed around and all that but never 'it'. Then after about two months' marriage she announces she's got preggers. Some nigger's, I thought to meself. Then along comes Baby Jason. She couldn't cope. She collapsed. She's a mess. Had to have the baby adopted. So you see, Mark, whatever your game is, I'm not your old man anyhow.

MARK: Whatever you say, Pop.

JEFFREY: Odd, isn't it? Me a traffic warden, her a dinner lady, you'd never think it. That we'd live like this. That this would happen to us. Who'd have thought? [*Pause.*] You're a fine boy. You've got potential. Pity you had to go in for all this business. What'll you do?

MARK: What?

JEFFREY: With all the stuff?

MARK: I've a room. This could furnish it nicely. Or I might sell. Make a few quid. I'm a privileged boy. Lucky. A boy whose parents will set him up. Give him his own home.

JEFFREY: Don't talk daft. I'll go to the law, mind. I will.

MARK: Lilly Law! And what'll you say? That your missus got shafted by your son today and then you did. And then he stole your lives away. From under your very noses... Lilly will laugh. Think you're a crackpot. Anyhow, do as you please. You shan't see me again.

JEFFREY: I'm disappointed in you, son. Whoever you are, I'm disappointed. Mind you, I'm a disappointed man. I once came to that orphanage. St. Theresa's. You'd have been about three or four. It was after 'She Loves You' came out. Remember I said. Gave me a new lease of life. I thought, I'll go and see Baby Jason. He's young. Needn't know who I am. They let me. The authorities let me. You were playing with this big yellow truck. Didn't have no wheels. There was this other little boy. Sullen type. Kept on following you, he did. Never stopped. And you never took no notice. Followed you all around that room. He was an intense sort. And you never took no notice. Pushed that yellow truck round and round. No wheels. Made a scraping noise. And I just stood in the corner and stared, and I thought, 'Blimey, they're a disturbed lot, these kids. Troubled.' I left. Not long after, I became a traffic warden.

MARK: That was our Michael. Not so intense. He's always followed me. I hated it there. Never forgive you for that, Pop. Never forgive.

JEFFREY: I seen folks bring up their kids. Plenty of money, all the privileges, they still hate each other. What's the difference?

MARK: Is that why you did it? Put me in there? 'Cos it makes no difference in the end. I knew it was you. When you come to St. Theresa's. Sensed you was there. Kids know and all, mind. I remember you in the corner, staring, you looked terrified. You was crying, wasn't you, Pop? All too much for ya. You're my old man all right. Crying for your own flesh and blood. She's no whore. I been following her. Never picks no-one up. You're the one who pulls the boys. Pulling them then, were you? That why she cracked up?

JEFFREY: Who are you anyway? Coming in here. [*shouting*] Who are you? Bloody imposter. I never slept with her. I never fathered no children.

MARK: I was pushing the truck but I knew you was there. Just 'cos you turned out to be a queer, no need to be ashamed, Pop. Could have brought a kid up queer and all.

JEFFREY: [*shouting*] Who the fuck are you?

MARK: That's it. Get it out the system. You'll feel more normal then.

JEFFREY: What have you come here for? [*Pause.*] Why now? [*Pause.*] Why have you come here now? After all these years? I never wanted to give you away. I could have brought you up. Properly. Decently. It was her. She's too bloody neurotic. Let me help you now, son. Let me make amends, eh? [*Pause.*] Eh? [*Pause.*] What have you come here for?

MARK: I've come for what's mine. What's rightly mine. We all have to pay for our crimes in life, Dad.

[JANINE *and* MICHAEL *enter.*]

JANINE: A most enjoyable experience. You don't mind, do you, Jace? You're not embarrassed by your old Mum. I say, it's looking quite bare in here. We'll have to redecorate.

MICHAEL: What? Whose old Mum?

JANINE: Me, of course. Jason's Mum.

MICHAEL: What?

MARK: Get packing, Michael!

MICHAEL: She's your Mum?

JEFFREY: Course she bloody ain't.

MICHAEL: [*dawning*] Paternal chat. Got my smile. Blimey, you never said.

MARK: Yes, well, leave it, all right?

MICHAEL: I never knew, honest. Bit of crumpet and fifty quid, that's all.

JEFFREY: Bit of crumpet! Bloody cheek. Fifty quid! That what he's paying you? Petty thief.

MICHAEL: I never knew. I'm fond of your missus. We'd made an arrangement. She's gonna let me call her Aunty. Mind if I call you Unc?

JEFFREY: You're bloody daft, boy. Being deceived all round. You want to see a doctor. Get a prescription.

MICHAEL: We'll make it a ritual, then. I'll come on a Sunday. Sunday tea. Lunch if you like.

MARK: Get on, Michael!

MICHAEL: You don't want to go treating them bad. Your own folk. You've got good folk here. I've been happy here.

MARK: Get on!

MICHAEL: I'll see to the cases, then. Yeah. He never said.
[*He removes the remaining luggage.*]

JANINE: Who is Mikey, Jason? Who is he? He's been a nice friend to you.

MARK: He was at the home. Older boy. Bit of a pet, really. But he's a decent bloke. Kept outa trouble. When it come time for him to leave the home, he stayed on as a paid helper. Worked in the gardens. Decent wages, mind. Got green fingers, he have. He's been good to me. Follers me round. He's the type of bloke that can hold down a job. He doesn't say much. But he's a reliable bloke. Kept outa trouble.

JEFFREY: In...bloody...deed. Soft in the nut.

JANINE: You sent him into that park? Sent him here this morning?

MARK: Checking the coast. No harm.

JANINE: Oh! I've a debt to you, then.

MARK: He's a reliable bloke. I told you.

JANINE: I told him he can come round. Call on a Sunday.

JEFFREY: Over my dead body.

[MICHAEL *enters.*]

JANINE: We just been hearing all about you, Mikey. Jason gives you a good reference. Says you're reliable.

MICHAEL: I am. I'd the cubic footage of this room worked out to a millimetre. Yeah. Inside me own head.

JANINE: You know, Mikey, when you mentioned the interview for Removal Man it never dawned you were holding the interview with me. You're a one!

JEFFREY: Shut up, woman. Can't you see — he's a common thief. Raping and pilfering. They're a couple of wide boys.

JANINE: You're bitter and twisted, Jeffrey, that's your problem.

MICHAEL: I'll just take the hi-fi, then. Yeah.

JANINE: All right, Mikey, you get on. Don't take no notice.

MICHAEL: I'll be aiming to pop in on you again, Missus. Yeah. Of a free afternoon.

JANINE: All right, Mikey, you do that.

[MICHAEL *removes the stereo.*]

MICHAEL: He never mentioned nothing.

JEFFREY: You going to stand by and watch your own mother make a whore of herself?

MARK: Leave off, Dad. That's between you and Mum... and Michael.

JANINE: Don't come over all precious, Jeffrey. I've slept with all the boys in this room.

JEFFREY: You slept with all the boys in the whole bloody school when we was courting. 'Cept me. Don't know what I had to go and mix with you for.

JANINE: I was the only belle who'd have you.

JEFFREY: Some belle.

JANINE: I was your only friend.

MARK: Now then, folks, hate to interrupt, but it's time we were down to the undies.

JEFFREY: What are you on about?

MARK: Strip!

JANINE: Oh no, Jason. A frolic with Mikey was one thing. But not with my own flesh and blood. Not now that I know. That would be incest. Terrible.

MARK: Just get 'em off, all right?

JANINE: 'Course Jace, anything you say.

MARK: [*brandishing the knife*] And you, Pop.

JEFFREY: You want a bit of dignity in your life. Let me make amends, eh?

MARK: Save the platitudes for the beat.

>   [JANINE *and* JEFFREY *strip to their under-*
>   *wear.*]

It's been a fine day. I've enjoyed meself. Quite an outing. I hope I've given you some pleasure. I would hate to think that the youngsters today were just all take, take and more take. We've got to have a little give around here. And I think, in all fairness, we can safely say that you two have given more than your fair share. No son could have had a better start in life... And the watch.

>   [JEFFREY *hands over his clothes and watch,*
>   *as does* JANINE. MICHAEL *enters, having*
>   *cleared the stereo and luggage.*]

MICHAEL: Yeah. Well, that's everything, then. All except them pictures and the sofa. [*winking at* JANINE] And, of course, that bed.

JANINE: Oh, leave the bed, Jace. Leave the bed. Where'll me and Dad sleep?

MARK: Do what?

MICHAEL: Come on, then. We'd better get on. It's getting late.

[*He goes into the bedroom, followed by* MARK. JANINE *and* JEFFREY *sit on the remaining sofa in their underwear.*]

MARK: You'll be all right, wontcha?

[*He exits.*]

JANINE: Oooh, Dad, it's ever so big in here.

JEFFREY: Well, it would be.

JANINE: Why? It was never big before. This was never a large flat.

JEFFREY: It's empty now, you idiot.

JANINE: There you go. No need for rudeness. I am well aware that it's empty. I too am in the room. Undergoing this experience. It was thoughtful of them to leave this sofa.

JEFFREY: It's all your fault.

JANINE: What is?

JEFFREY: This. What's happening. This.

JANINE: I fail to see how.

JEFFREY: If you hadn't been such a tart. If you hadn't gone sleeping around. Getting pregnant.

JANINE: I think we might say you had something to do with my impregnation.

JEFFREY: No, I never. I never touched your lowers.

JANINE: You filthy liar. You never stopped touching them when we was newly married.

JEFFREY: I never did. We had grounds for annulment.

JANINE: You saying Baby Jason isn't yours?

JEFFREY: Precisely.

JANINE: Well, that's not true. You're a liar. Is that what you told him? You coward!

> [MARK *and* MICHAEL *enter from the bed-room, carrying the bed.*]

Here, Jason, you don't want to go listening to your Dad. His memory's failing. I was a virgin when we got married.

JEFFREY: You were never a virgin. Not ever. Virginity is a quality which bypassed your life.

MICHAEL: You got them rowing, now, see? They're nice folk. Don't want to get them rowing.

MARK: Shut up! Mind that bloody door.

> [MARK *and* MICHAEL *exit with the bed.*]

JANINE: What you want to go telling him lies for? Upsetting the boy.

JEFFREY: All right. Supposing it is Baby Jason. Supposing he is my son. I'm not letting him near you. You're not fit to be his mother. Tarting around. Our Jason deserves more than some old tart for a Mum.

JANINE: Oh, Dad. You've always had this notion that I slept around. I can count the number of men that I've slept with on one hand. And the majority's here now. I got pregnant the first time we did it. I never slept around. Not me. I used to pretend of a Tuesday. Keep you happy. I do believe Mikey was the first pick-up, Dad. Yes, I've been liberated since these boys put in an appearance. Liberated. It's getting quite nippy in here. I'll just slip me housecoat on. Oh! I say. I can't! They've packed it off.

JEFFREY: I curse the day I was married. My life's been

nothing but trouble. My old Mum begged me
not to marry you. Said you was common.

JANINE: She was a blind old baggage. Never went out of
the house. What would she know? I think we
should do this room blue, don't you? I've been
longing to redecorate. This is the perfect
opportunity. Life's an adventure, isn't it?

JEFFREY: I'm leaving you. I've had it. It's *decree nisi* for me
in the morning. I'm filing. I'm off. To think our
Jason's turned out to be the victim of a broken
marriage. A child of divorce.

[*He goes to the front door.*]

JANINE: You won't get far in them undies. I hope they
were clean on today. I hope you haven't
dribbled.

JEFFREY: Don't namby-pamby!

[MARK *and* MICHAEL *enter and remove the
sofa.*]

JANINE: Oh, calm down, lovey. Things aren't so bad.
We been through worse. 'Member that time we
went to Eastbourne and the train got stuck in
that tunnel for three hours? That was much
worse than this.

JEFFREY: Only 'cos you wouldn't stop rabbiting. Everyone in the whole bloody train was staring at us.
It was totally bloody humiliating.

JANINE: Yes, it was much worse than this.

JEFFREY: I don't know why I bloody married you.

JANINE: You married me 'cos your Mum went and died.
Good riddance. You were on your tod. No
bloody family. No one to look after you. So you
married me. Now, let's hear no more of that.

JEFFREY: You've made my entire life a living bloody
misery.

JANINE: Don't talk rot. You spend more time in toilets than most blokes. Oh, I am looking forward to getting started on this flat.

JEFFREY: I'm not bringing him up with you for his mother. I'd sooner kill meself. I'm going to kill meself. I am. I'm going to kill meself.

[*He sticks his head in the oven.*]

JANINE: Calm down, Jeffrey, you'll give us all a headache. Besides, that cooker's electrical. Here. I bet we could claim on the Insurance. We could say we come home from the pictures and found the whole place stripped bare.

[MARK *and* MICHAEL *enter and start to roll up the carpet.*]

JEFFREY: We're going to look a bit bloody daft wandering into the Insurance in our bloody knickers.

JANINE: Don't be so pessimistic. I'll steal washing off the lines. Here, Jace, it's obvious you didn't inherit your imagination off your old Dad.

JEFFREY: [*to* JANINE] Fuck off! Fuck off out of here and leave our Jace alone.

[MICHAEL *drops the carpet he is removing.*]

MICHAEL: Hey! Don't be upset, Uncle. Come down the pub. We'll have a jar.

MARK: Pick up this bleeding carpet, you idiot!

MICHAEL: It's a crying shame. Your own father.

[MARK *and* MICHAEL *exit with the carpet.*]

JANINE: Dad, calm down. You'll have the whole of West Hampstead in here. Here, come and sit down. He's a nice boy, that Michael.

[*She sits in the centre of the bare floor.* JEFFREY *moves towards her.*]

JEFFREY: I suppose. Our Jason needs parental guidance. He needs a real father! [*with rising hysteria*] My life's a mess. I hate that job. Hate it. The way you get treated. This bloke today. Parked on the pavement, he did, and a double yeller. I said, "I'm sorry, sir, you'll have to move on." Told me to F. off, he did. I said, "Hey, I don't have to take that from you. I'm only doing my job. I'll have you clamped." Before you could turn round he'd gone. They're completely bloody terrified. Terrified of them clamps. Mention them clamps and they think you're Pope. Best thing that ever happened to bloody England, them clamps are. I hate that job.

[*He falls to the floor, broken.*]

JANINE: You take things too serious. I'll get some fresh cornflakes in the morning. When the boys are done you have a hot bath. I've hidden the Fairy Liquid, and I'll put the heating on, keep us nice and warm. They can't take the central.

[MARK *and* MICHAEL *enter.*]

MARK: Sorry to keep you. Didn't mean to be rude. All done now.

JEFFREY: Don't mention it. You've got impressive manners for a kid of your age. Makes me and your Mum proud.

MICHAEL: I'll say cheerio, then. Yeah.

JANINE: Oh, cheerio, Mikey. Good luck with the Removals.

MICHAEL: Oh, yeah. I get nervy. Nervy with a new job. I have worked Removals once before, mind. Stood me in good stead for today, eh?

JANINE: You're versatile in your trades.

MICHAEL: I'll say. I'll be seeing you, then.

[JANINE *kisses* MICHAEL *on the cheek.*]

JANINE: I do hope so.

MICHAEL: Of a Sunday. Sorry about all this. I've always done what he's told me, see? Been a mate to me, he have.

[JEFFREY *shakes* MICHAEL *by the hand.*]

JEFFREY: It's only natural. For a poor orphan boy. Like yourself. [*Pause.*] Sunday tea.

[*Pause.*]

MICHAEL: Sunday tea. See you in the van, Jace. All right. Yeah.

MARK: Here. Take them posters.

[MICHAEL *exits with the posters.*]

I'll take my leave. You've been great hosts. Made a good impression on Michael. Anyway, 'nuff said. By the way, I'll leave you this. A little token. The Beatles. Never liked them myself. Love is all you need!

[*He throws down a cassette in front of them. He makes to leave, then he turns back.*]

Funny to see you two sitting there like that. But there you are, that's life. You're walking along and you see this old tramp crossing the road. He's got a funny walk, bit of a limp and he uses this very gnarled old piece of wood as a stick. There's snot running down his nose and his nose is so red and bulbous he looks like he was born an alcoholic. He's got a few wisps of hair and one eye seems to be lower than the other. He's carrying bags all over the place. Carrying, all his life. And I think if I walked into the cinema now and he was up on the screen I'd go, "Get off, what a load of old fanny!" But there you are…that's life! Be lucky!

[*He is gone.* JANINE *turns to* JEFFREY.]

JANINE: Our Jason's turned out deep.

JEFFREY: He's a boy with intellect. Objective.
          [*He gets up.*]
          Here. Fancy a quick Cherry B down the pub?
          [JANINE *gets up.*]
JANINE: Oh, I say. What a treat. I love treats.
          [*They stand facing each other in the centre of the room.*]
          [*The lights fade to total darkness.*]

THE END